No More Word Searches

By Bob Watson

© 2015

Introduction

Learning is an active pursuit.

No matter how you want to spin an activity, it requires a student to do or complete something in order to learn it. The active element might be something simple like an impromptu speech or a basic worksheet, or it may be complex, like a portfolio assignment or a research paper. It could be artistic like a drawing or sculpture, or it could be a science experiment. No matter what it is, students have to be doing something in order to learn material well.

Year after year, I purchase, review, and make use of dozens of new classroom resources all promising new active elements of learning. Most of them are very useful, and some of them become all-stars on my shelf of go-to activities. Only a few get trashed. Some of them are guides to research projects, others are simple worksheets, others are based on contemporary classroom reading novels, like The Outsiders or The Giver. They are from a wide range of subject areas, disciplines, age levels, and ability levels. In fact, they really only have one thing in common: Word Searches.

If you haven't been able to guess from the title of this book, I absolutely HATE word searches.

I've worked in many schools, and in my current role, I talk with many different teachers every day. I've seen word searches appear all over the place, from the early kindergarten classrooms where students are first putting letters together, to AP Psychology for Seniors in high school, where fundamental theories of personalities have been wrapped into squarish blocks of random letters.

Sometimes, when I'm feeling a little plucky, I'll ask teachers why they include them.

"They're fun," say many of the kindergarten and early grade teachers, as if they can't come up with a simple art project that will let the kids learn to express themselves while having a blast.

"It's a break from the usual activities," say some of the middle grade teachers, who don't seem to realize that many of their colleagues are all using the same kinds of materials.

"They have to learn the words somehow," say English and Language arts teachers who are concerned with vocabulary, not realizing that I could just as easily search for any three-letter piece of the word and solve the puzzle without spelling any of the actual words. And it sure doesn't teach meaning.

"It teaches spelling," is a common excuse I've heard from teachers at all levels, yet it really doesn't. In more than 97% of all word searches, it takes only a combination of ANY three-letter piece of a word to identify the unique placement of that word. In other words, if I wanted to find the word "useless" in a word search, I could look for "use" or "ele" or "ess" and if I were to find one of those letter segments, I have found the entire word more than 97% of the time. There are obvious exceptions: had the words "useless" and "elephant" appeared in the same word search, I wouldn't have been able to uniquely identify one or the other based on "ele" because they both contain the same string, but in real life, most word searchers would have honed in on a rarer pattern like the double-s at the end of useless or the "ph" in elephant.

In fact, through talking with literally hundreds of teachers, dozens of administrators, and thousands of students, I have yet to hear a single valid argument about the benefit of doing word searches in a classroom, with one notable exception:

"Sometimes you have to fill time."

There's an excuse that you really don't want to hear from teachers, who are already complaining about not having enough instructional time to make it through a whole year's curriculum in the time they have, yet it keeps cropping up.

As a former classroom teacher, I have to admit, there is a lot of dead time that could be filled. Think about that lull after handing out a test, when your "hare" students have already scribbled their way through the material while other "tortoise" students are taking their time and working through the material methodically. Or how about those times when an administrator interrupts your class for a phone call or a one-on-one conference with an angry parent that needs to happen immediately. What about after an unexpected scuffle inside the classroom, or the ten minutes after the movie has stopped playing, but before the bell for next class rings?

So why not a word search then? Because there's something better.

What you have in this book is that better alternative. This book, *No More Word Searches*, contains over forty different word puzzles that teach strategy, vocabulary, rhyme, and creativity, while fostering opportunities for partnering with others, or competition. They are difficult enough to provide a challenge for all ages (even some AP students in 12th grade), yet simple enough that students as young as 3rd or 4th grade have managed to complete them, albeit with some difficulty.

These puzzles can help you fill the gaps of time. You could use them to teach strategy and vocabulary. Younger students might benefit from using the internet or books to research some of the cultural or idiomatic clues. At my current position, I use them as rewards to encourage my students to finish their work and do well on tests. They can be adapted and modified easily using the templates at the back of the book to provide engaging vocabulary worksheets.

These logic puzzles may not necessarily fit within the Common Core or State Standards which must guide your practice, but they are a phenomenal way to engage your classroom, reward your students, and give a little levity to your class without bringing in any word searches.

What's in this Book?

Well, you've already read the introduction, so hopefully you're excited to start puzzling your way through the rest.

There are four other sections in this book: the descriptions, the puzzles, the answer keys, and the blank templates.

The first deals with a description of the puzzles, as well as including information about how the clues are used, and the best strategy for solving them. This section also gives you a few details of how you can use extension activities to further explore the games. Extension activities are often more difficult versions of the original games, but might also include whole-class activities or more in-depth looks at strategy.

The puzzles are the actual reproducables that you can use in your classroom.

The answer keys give all of the answers, and are laid out in the order of the puzzles themselves.

The blank templates can be used to create your own versions of each of the games. Many teachers have found, for instance, that using the week's spelling or vocabulary words into their own version of the Lame Game is a great way to reinforce vocabulary skills.

Descriptions

Word Ladders

As the worksheet states, word ladders were initially created by Lewis Carroll (a mathematician, and author of the *Alice in Wonderland* novels). His initial idea was to give you a starting word and an ending word, and no clues in between. This is too difficult for most students.

The word ladders presented here follow a similar pattern – students get to see a starting word and an ending word, and have to fill in the remaining based on clues – changing only one letter at a time. Each successive word shares three letters with the previous to form a new word.

Strategy

It's possible to work from the top down or from the bottom up, which is useful if students get stuck on a particularly difficult clue.

Students will probably try to jump around at first, which they will soon see is not a particularly effective strategy unless they are an exceptional guesser. At most, it is recommended that they jump only one clue, using two letters from the original word and two new letters. If they can achieve this, it should be fairly easy to figure out the word that was initially skipped.

Some students will also try to figure words out using rhyming or alliteration, which is a somewhat useful strategy. After all, there is a 75% chance that the first letter does not change, and many words that share the final set of letters do rhyme. This is, of course, a strategy that is only occasionally useful, and something that will be completely ruined once they have graduated to Double Word Ladders.

Clues

The clues for the Word Ladders range from simple definitions ("Winter sporting equipment" for SKIS) to idioms ("There is no 'I' in this word" for "TEAM"). There are a few double entendres, puns and a few questions that ask about history or culture. Students who will be successful at these types of puzzles will need to display a wide variety of knowledge, and the ability to think about words in a variety of ways.

Extension: Word Pyramids

Word Pyramids involve adding letters to successive words to eventually create a 5-letter word. One letter starts the puzzle, and then a single letter is added to create a two-letter word. A third letter is added after this, sometimes requiring scrambling of the letters. The pattern continues for four and five letter words. A clue is provided for each successive step to make it a little easier. These are more challenging for many students, but not so difficult as the Double Word Ladders.

Extension: Double Word Ladders

Why stop with changing only one letter? The Double Word Ladders collection in this guide have the same principle as the single, changing two letters per line instead of just one. This simple change makes these puzzles significantly more difficult for students to complete, and often ruins many of the less useful strategies from single word ladders, especially the use of rhyming words and alliteration. Use these for students who have mastered the first eight Word Ladders.

The Lame Game

The Lame Game was named by one of my students. It's very clever – the answer to each question is a two-word rhyming phrase.

The phrases may be commonplace ("creature feature") but the vast majority are nonsense phrases ("Fruit boot") and oftentimes the clues are written as two synonyms. A partial word bank on the bottom of each worksheet keeps these from being impossible for students, but the most you'll get for any one question is half of the answer. The other must always be provided by the student.

Strategy

To complete the Lame Games without using the word bank, the strategy has to be to first extract the two separate ideas that are given in the clue. Most of the time, this is not too difficult ("A flying fantasy creature who needs a shave" has two parts: the "flying fantasy creature", and the "needs a shave"); although there are some tricky ones thrown in throughout ("Minimalist art containing one-dimensional shapes" uses "Minimalist" and "one-dimensional shapes" to refer to "line" and only "art" to refer to "design"). Without identifying the two pieces of the clue word, the Lame Game is very difficult.

With the word bank, it is most likely that students can identify half of the clues very quickly. The word bank shifts back and forth between adjectives and nouns, so placement can be difficult, especially on noun-noun clues, but with identification of the second-half of the answer, it is usually not too difficult for students to figure out the answers.

Clues

Because of the nature of the Lame Game, most of the answers are nonsensical. There is no such thing as a "witty city" or "emu stew," making these kinds of clues straightforward vocabulary questions. If you can identify "an urban locale" as a "city" and "funny" as a synonym for "witty," then you've got it.

The clues which refer to things that could exist are often much more difficult. Some, like "foundry boundary," follow the same pattern as before –the "edge" is the "boundary" and the "steel mill" is the "foundry," but most of these clues are more difficult to find the hints for the specific words.

Extension: The Galling Game

The Lame Game can be used to teach many types of Figurative Language, but perhaps the easiest one is demonstrated by the Galling Game. The Galling Game is similar to the Lame Game in that the answers are all two-word clues, though this time all of the answers are alliterative instead of rhyming. Students have typically found the Galling Game more difficult than the Lame Game.

Word Squares

Word Squares are word searches that makes you think.

Word Squares were born from the game Boggle™, one of my all-time favorite games. You search the puzzles for words, using tiles adjacent or diagonal to one another to form words. Each letter must be connected to the next, and no letters can be repeated in the same word. For each puzzle, a category is specified to help guide students towards specific words.

Of all the puzzles, this is probably the most difficult to complete. Most students will be able to find half to three-quarters of the words, and may have a great deal of difficulty finding the remaining words.

Strategy

There are two strategies that you can use to solve the puzzles: thinking about the category to find the words, or looking at the puzzles to generate words.

Thinking about the category is probably the most useful. If the clue is "things you'd find on a calendar" you could check for individual month names, day names, the words "day", "month", "year" and "holiday". Maybe check for the names of some individual holidays if you need more.

Looking at the puzzle to generate words is more difficult, but can work once you've exhausted your original list of words. Finding "th" next to each other might prompt a search for words including that pair of letters, for instance.

Clues

The clues for the Word Square puzzles are categories. There are some general categories ("Types of Pasta"), as well as a few historical ones ("Recent Presidents") and a few that could fit into units in science ("Birds" or "Outer Space"). The most important skill for this puzzle is the ability to think of a wide variety of words that fit within a particular category.

Extension: In-Class Boggle™ Game

Using an overhead projector or document reader, it is simple to create your own Boggle™ game that can be played as an in-class activity. Challenge students to find longer words, and to use the strategies that they may have used doing Lame Games and Word Ladders to find patterns within the board – often multiple words can be found using rhyming patterns (CAN, PAN, FAN) or beginnings (CAN, CAP, CAR).

Extension: Spelling Challenge

Creating your own Word Squares is not all particularly difficult, especially when dealing with lists of spelling words, which often test a student's ability to create words with similar endings. A word square can easily be created for a list of ten to fifteen spelling words using the template in the back of this book, and it can function as a much more interesting way to introduce a new list of spelling words than a pre-test.

Missing Letter Puzzles

Missing Letter puzzles ask you to figure out the many different uses a single letter can have.

Each Puzzle includes a pie diagram, each slice of the pie containing two or three letters. Each slice of the pie can, with the addition of a single letter, form a new word. The challenge of the student is to figure out which letter they need to add in order to make a new word in every single pie slice.

The letters in each slice of pie can be scrambled, and may need to be rearranged in order to make the new words. There is only one solution to each and every puzzle.

Strategy

Missing Letter Puzzles are designed to show students the many different ways each letter can be used. The missing letter will start and end words, and may be found within the word as well. Some pie slices can make multiple words.

The best strategy for this puzzle is the focus on a single pair of words, usually those that you may think can make the fewest possible words. For instance, one puzzle has pie slices including "YE" and "FL". The "ye" pair can make "yes," "yen," "key," "hey" and "eye" only. The "FL" can only make "elf," and "fly." Finding the "e" in both of those words is a clear indication that this is the missing letter, and checking it with the other pie slices will verify that this is true.

The three-letter puzzles are generally very straightforward, and the four-letter puzzles are more challenging. Each worksheet contains one of each.

Clues

Care was taken in the creation of these puzzles to make certain that the missing letters are used in every position of the word. There are no puzzles, for instance, where the letter is used only as the first or last letter. Because of this, many puzzles have some difficult words.

Extension: Missing Numbers

Teachers of World or American History courses can modify the missing letter puzzles to make missing number puzzles. Significant historical events in the United States happened in 1492 (Columbus sets sail to discover America), 1590 (the abandoned Roanoke Colony was found), 1692 (Salem Witch Trials began), 1789 (The Constitution replaced the Articles of Confederation), 1889 (Montana became a state), 1913 (Income Tax Amendment was added to the Constitution), and 1993 (The World Trade Center was bombed). Each of these dates includes a "9". Clues will have to be given for almost all of these, but it can be a good fact-finding activity for younger students, and a significant memory challenge for students in higher grade levels.

The Puzzles

Word Ladders #1

Word ladder puzzles were invented by Lewis Carroll, the author of Alice in Wonderland, among other books. These kinds of puzzles are designed to test your vocabulary and reasoning skills. In each puzzle, you must change just one letter from the line above to create a new word that fits the clue. The first one is started for you.

T O A D	A leaping amphibian
_ O A D	A street
_ _ _ _	To examine a written work
_ _ _ _	Towards the back
_ _ _ _	Phobias
_ _ _ _	Achievement
_ _ _ _	Level or smooth
_ _ _ _	Banner
_ _ _ N	A Spanish Dessert
_ _ _ _	The closing part of an envelope
_ _ _ _	A strike with an open hand
_ _ _ _	To Fall
_ _ _ _	Skinny
_ _ _ _	To read quickly
_ _ _ _	A piece of sporting equipment
_ _ _ _	A short role-play
_ _ _ _	To expel liquid from your mouth
S P I N	To turn around

Word Ladders #2

Word ladder puzzles were invented by Lewis Carroll, the author of Alice in Wonderland, among other books. These kinds of puzzles are designed to test your vocabulary and reasoning skills. In each puzzle, you must change just one letter from the line above to create a new word that fits the clue. The first one is started for you.

L O A N	To borrow money
L O A _	A heavy burden
_ _ _ _	Ruler of a country or nation
_ _ _ _	Fat used in cooking
_ _ _ _	Something you send someone
_ _ _ _	A wire
_ _ _ _	The opposite of sweltering
_ _ _ _	To put away laundry
_ _ _ _	A car company, or crossing a river
_ _ _ _	Yell this before swinging in golf
_ _ _ _	Long ago (in days of _____)
_ _ _ _	A city in England
_ _ _ _	Eating utensil
_ _ _ _	A type of board
_ _ _ _	A yellow vegetable
_ _ _ _	Early in the day
_ _ _ _	Keep it coming
C O R E	The center

Word Ladders #3

Word ladder puzzles were invented by Lewis Carroll, the author of Alice in Wonderland, among other books. These kinds of puzzles are designed to test your vocabulary and reasoning skills. In each puzzle, you must change just one letter from the line above to create a new word that fits the clue. The first one is started for you.

F E E L	What you do with emotion
F E E _	Attached to your ankles
_ _ _ _	A type of fabric
_ _ _ _	What ice does
_ _ _ _	To put two ideas together
_ _ _ _	It grows on old vegetables
_ _ _ _	I _____ you yesterday!
_ _ _ _	Frosty
_ _ _ _	Nursery rhyme (Old King....)
_ _ _ _	A type of drink
_ _ _ _	Hello in Spanish
_ _ _ _	Grasp
_ _ _ _	Used to grasp
_ _ _ _	Your uppermost body part
_ _ _ _	It used to be in paint
_ _ _ _	The faucet might do this
_ _ _ _	A bird's mouth
B E A N	A Legume

Word Ladders #4

Word ladder puzzles were invented by Lewis Carroll, the author of Alice in Wonderland, among other books. These kinds of puzzles are designed to test your vocabulary and reasoning skills. In each puzzle, you must change just one letter from the line above to create a new word that fits the clue. The first one is started for you.

C L O T	Something your blood could form
_ L O T	A place you put mail
_ _ _ _	What pigs eat
_ _ _ _	To strike with an open hand
_ _ _ _	Applaud
_ _ _ _	Worn (like armor)
_ _ _ _	Happy
_ O _ _	To Encourage
_ _ _ _	A four-legged farm animal
_ _ _ _	The river around a castle
_ _ _ _	When a bird loses feathers
_ _ _ _	To form
_ _ _ _	A small rodent, or a facial feature
_ _ _ _	Something you could fall in
_ _ _ _	An aspiration
_ _ _ _	To solve problems yourself
_ _ _ _	Superman wears this
C A P S	Baseball players wear them

Word Ladders #5

Word ladder puzzles were invented by Lewis Carroll, the author of Alice in Wonderland, among other books. These kinds of puzzles are designed to test your vocabulary and reasoning skills. In each puzzle, you must change just one letter from the line above to create a new word that fits the clue. The first one is started for you.

B O O K	Literature
B O O _	A piece of footwear
_ _ _ _	A strike of lightning
_ _ _ _	It holds up your pants
_ _ _ _	A mark from injury
_ _ _ _	A place to draw water from
_ _ _ _	To receive money for something
_ _ _ _	A marine animal
_ _ _ _	A shade of blue
_ _ _ _	There's no "I" in this word
_ _ _ _	A monorail
_ _ _ _	A small measure of weight
_ _ _ _	Halfway between white and black
_ _ _ _	What your food comes on
_ _ _ _	You might lay one of these
_ _ _ _	To fall down
_ _ _ _	Gloves improve your _____
G R I M	A bad outlook

Word Ladders #6

Word ladder puzzles were invented by Lewis Carroll, the author of Alice in Wonderland, among other books. These kinds of puzzles are designed to test your vocabulary and reasoning skills. In each puzzle, you must change just one letter from the line above to create a new word that fits the clue. The first one is started for you.

R O C K	Stone
_ O C K	Something you wear on your foot
_ _ _ _	A bag
_ _ _ _	A type of Nordstrom's store
_ _ _ _	The turtle won this
_ _ _ _	Doilies are made out of this
_ _ _ _	If you have an injured foot
_ _ _ _	Small green fruit
_ _ _ _	Sagging
_ _ _ _	Someone cowardly
_ _ _ _	So thin and light you can't see it
_ _ _ _	A yellowjacket
_ _ _ _	To clean
_ _ _ _	A colorful belt
_ _ _ _	Someone spunky has this
_ _ _ _	To throw a ball to a teammate
_ _ _ _	Long ago
M A S T	Where a ship's sail hangs

Word Ladders #7

Word ladder puzzles were invented by Lewis Carroll, the author of Alice in Wonderland, among other books. These kinds of puzzles are designed to test your vocabulary and reasoning skills. In each puzzle, you must change just one letter from the line above to create a new word that fits the clue. The first one is started for you.

L E T S	To Lease
_ E T S	A New York Football Team
_ _ _ _	Sticks out
_ _ _ _	No ifs, ands or ...
_ _ _ _	Hamburgers have two of them
_ _ _ _	A way to hit a baseball
_ _ _ _	Crooked
_ _ _ _	A place to sleep
_ _ _ _	To care for
_ _ _ _	To care for an injury
_ _ _ _	Opposite of Womens
_ _ _ _	Kids make this
_ _ _ _	Force = _____ x Acceleration
_ _ _ _	To toss a football
_ _ _ _	Long ago (in the _____)
_ _ _ _	The farthest behind
_ _ _ _	To Desire
J U S T	Fair

Word Ladders #8

Word ladder puzzles were invented by Lewis Carroll, the author of Alice in Wonderland, among other books. These kinds of puzzles are designed to test your vocabulary and reasoning skills. In each puzzle, you must change just one letter from the line above to create a new word that fits the clue. The first one is started for you.

S A L T	It used to be used as money
S A L _	When prices go down
_ _ _ _	Just alike
_ _ _ _	Everyone has one
_ _ _ _	A city in Alaska
_ _ _ _	Zero
_ _ _ _	A pointed cylinder
_ _ _ _	Old people often need this
_ _ _ _	Cannot
_ _ _ _	Your dog does this to sweat
_ _ _ _	Piece
_ _ _ _	Where ships come in
_ _ _ _	Where soldiers used to stay
_ _ _ _	An eating utensil
_ _ _ _	People, or Woodie Guthrie's music
_ _ _ _	A former, unremarkable president
_ _ _ _	The earth has two of these
R O L E	The part you play

Double Word Ladders #1

Word ladder puzzles were invented by Lewis Carroll, the author of Alice in Wonderland, among other books. These kinds of puzzles are designed to test your vocabulary and reasoning skills. In each puzzle, you must change two of the letters from the line above to create a new word that fits the clue. The first one is started for you.

H A R D	Not soft
H _ _ D	To grasp
H _ _ _	Important piece of armor
_ E _ P	A type of seaweed
_ _ _ _	They come on a ring
_ _ _ _	Sunlight arrives through…
_ _ _ _	A type of precipitation
_ _ _ _	Another type of precipitation
_ _ _ _	You can do this from a height
_ _ _ _	Not a girl
_ _ _ _	The opposite of spicy
_ _ _ _	A soft, smooth fabric
_ _ _ _	A type of fur coat
_ _ _ _	A lot
_ _ _ _	A part of a road
_ _ _ _	A rabbit
_ _ _ _	To sharpen
H O L D	To grasp

Double Word Ladders #2

Word ladder puzzles were invented by Lewis Carroll, the author of Alice in Wonderland, among other books. These kinds of puzzles are designed to test your vocabulary and reasoning skills. In each puzzle, you must change two of the letters from the line above to create a new word that fits the clue. The first one is started for you.

F O R K	An Eating Utensil
F O _ _	Something soft and squishy
_ _ _ _	Something you drive on
_ _ _ _	Happy
_ _ _ _	Something that seals
_ _ _ _	A mistake
_ _ _ _	A primary color
_ _ _ _	Verifiable
_ _ _ _	A trip around the world
_ _ _ _	Larger than a village
_ _ _ _	Farm animals
_ _ _ _	An indoor pet
_ _ _ _	Gloves
_ _ _ _	It comes from the farm animals
_ _ _ _	Become upset
_ _ _ _	A barn fixture
H A L O	Angels have them

Double Word Ladders #3

Word ladder puzzles were invented by Lewis Carroll, the author of Alice in Wonderland, among other books. These kinds of puzzles are designed to test your vocabulary and reasoning skills. In each puzzle, you must change two of the letters from the line above to create a new word that fits the clue. The first one is started for you.

S T A R	A celestial object
S _ A _	Part of a chair
_ _ _ T	It makes up the basin of the Nile
_ I _ _	This comes from farm animals
_ _ _ _	A flavor of chewing gum
_ _ _ _	It happens in a car wreck
_ _ _ _	Not right
_ _ _ _	Not hard
_ _ _ _	The opposite of bought
_ _ _ _	A young male horse
_ _ _ _	To sort laundry
_ _ _ _	Not spicy
_ _ _ _	Where you go shopping
_ _ _ _	Not a valley
_ _ _ _	Stop!
_ _ _ _	It happens to Ice
_ _ _ _	Something you eat
F E A R	A scared feeling

Double Word Ladders #4

Word ladder puzzles were invented by Lewis Carroll, the author of Alice in Wonderland, among other books. These kinds of puzzles are designed to test your vocabulary and reasoning skills. In each puzzle, you must change two of the letters from the line above to create a new word that fits the clue. The first one is started for you.

H O P E	Something you do for the future
_ O P _	Police
_ _ _ _	Baby dogs
_ _ _ _	Yank
_ _ _ _	Where the farmer lived
_ _ _ _	Used to feel
_ _ _ _	Attached to your Ankle
_ _ _ _	Vile or nasty
M A _ _	A large hammer
_ _ _ _	What Magellan would use
_ _ _ _	A rabbit does this
_ _ _ _	House
_ _ _ _	A type of bunny
_ _ _ _	To create
_ _ _ _	A creature that brings inspiration
_ _ _ _	It grows on rocks
_ _ _ _	Wet, humid, visible air
K I S S	A colorful rock band

Double Word Ladders #5

Word ladder puzzles were invented by Lewis Carroll, the author of Alice in Wonderland, among other books. These kinds of puzzles are designed to test your vocabulary and reasoning skills. In each puzzle, you must change two of the letters from the line above to create a new word that fits the clue. The first one is started for you.

C O A T	Jacket
C O _ _	Frosty
C _ _ _	A word that goes with Index
_ _ _ _	A distinguishing sign
_ _ _ _	Mud
_ _ _ _	To drop into water
_ _ _ _	Every kitchen has one
_ _ _ _	He takes a seat
_ _ _ _	Horses eat these
_ _ _ _	A mistake
_ _ _ _	A Lasso
R _ _ L	A way of boiling
_ _ _ _	Part of a boat
_ _ _ _	One of the Beatles
_ _ _ _	You wear two of these, not one
_ _ _ _	Your Mother's Sister
_ _ _ _	Phoenix's Basketball Team
M U M S	An Autumn Flower

Double Word Ladders #6

Word ladder puzzles were invented by Lewis Carroll, the author of Alice in Wonderland, among other books. These kinds of puzzles are designed to test your vocabulary and reasoning skills. In each puzzle, you must change two of the letters from the line above to create a new word that fits the clue. The first one is started for you.

M I T E	A bedbug
M _ _ E	A Lion's Collar
_ _ _ _	Cupboard food container
_ _ _ _	To stay overnight, outdoors
_ _ _ _	A bump on a log
_ _ _ _	A complete circuit
_ _ _ _	Thunder's Noise
_ _ _ _	These hold up your roof
_ _ _ _	Greatest
_ _ _ _	If you don't wash your car, you get
_ _ _ _	An undesirable dog
_ _ _ _	Target and Wal-_____
_ _ _ _	Jelly comes in this
_ _ _ _	Airplanes
_ _ _ _	Short for Elizabeth
_ _ _ _	To smash in
_ _ _ _	Having no hair
B I R D	A flying animal

Double Word Ladders #7

Word ladder puzzles were invented by Lewis Carroll, the author of Alice in Wonderland, among other books. These kinds of puzzles are designed to test your vocabulary and reasoning skills. In each puzzle, you must change two of the letters from the line above to create a new word that fits the clue. The first one is started for you.

F L O O D	Noah survived one
_ L O O _	Standing Apart
_ _ _ _ _	By yourself
_ _ _ _ _	A Rock
_ _ _ _ _	After a bee gets you, you've been..
_ _ _ _ _	The opposite of Old
_ _ _ _ _	This is wasted on the young
_ _ _ _ _	There are twelve of these a year
_ _ _ _ _	Gum's flavor
_ _ _ _ _	Four cups makes two...
_ _ _ _ _	Pieces of cars
_ _ _ _ _	Like when a child cries
_ _ _ _ _	Mickey's dog, or an ex-planet
_ _ _ _ _	Food comes on these
_ _ _ _ _	A thing you might tie to your foot
_ _ _ _ _	A shovel, or a suit of cards
_ _ _ _ _	Potatoes
S O U L S	Everyone has one

Double Word Ladders #8

Word ladder puzzles were invented by Lewis Carroll, the author of Alice in Wonderland, among other books. These kinds of puzzles are designed to test your vocabulary and reasoning skills. In each puzzle, you must change two of the letters from the line above to create a new word that fits the clue. The first one is started for you.

S T Y L E	Your specific fashion
S T _ L _	Tranquil, peaceful
_ _ _ _ _	How you might describe a board
_ _ _ _ _	A rocky edge
_ _ _ _ _	The act of surmounting
_ _ _ _ _	This might put you in jail
_ _ _ _ _	To complain
_ _ _ _ _	Catholics say it before meals
_ _ _ _ _	Something a train runs on
_ _ _ _ _	How you'd describe gravy
_ _ _ _ _	To express gratitude
_ _ _ _ _	A noise a robot might make
_ _ _ _ _	Fast shutting of your eyes
_ _ _ _ _	David's weapon of choice
_ _ _ _ _	Goo
_ _ _ _ _	Something you might like to pass
_ _ _ _ _	Lasers shoot them
J E A N S	Levi's

The Lame Game #1

What's a fun activity you might not want to do? A "Lame Game." Answer each of the following clues below using two rhyming words. Some hints are provided, along with a partial word bank that provides half of the answer to each question.

1. A Novel about pork chops.	Cook	Book
2. A banana you wear on your foot.	_____	Boot
3. An imaginary flying creature who needs a shave.	Hairy	_____
4. An improved correspondence.	_____	_____
5. A boring story.	_____	_____
6. Where the amphibians live.	_____	_____
7. An intelligent cardiovascular organ.	_____	_____
8. If someone were to give you their cell.	_____	_____
9. A quiet presenter.	_____	_____
10. A paid-off loan.	_____	_____
11. A teacher puts it in her pencil to grade homework.	_____	_____
12. A very calm guy.	_____	_____
13. A bird with a degree in law.	_____	_____
14. What you'd call the pattern on your kitchen floor.	_____	_____
15. An odorous home.	_____	_____
16. A large group of cattle.	_____	_____
17. An engaging argument.	_____	_____
18. What a dolphin might wear at night-time.	_____	_____

Partial word bank:

flipper, phone, letter, crew, speaker, eagle, red, smelling, stale, debt, style, bog, smart, mellow, great

The Lame Game #2

What's a fun activity you might not want to do? A "Lame Game." Answer each of the following clues below using two rhyming words. Some hints are provided, along with a partial word bank that provides half of the answer to each question

1. A happy fruit.	Merry	Berry
2. What you'd use to protect things inside your dresser.	Sock	_____
3. A happy father.	_____	Dad
4. Soup made out of a large bird.	_____	_____
5. A place where the temperature is raised.	_____	_____
6. The ketchup that you spilled on your clothes.	_____	_____
7. A percussion instrument from the bad side of town.	_____	_____
8. An African deer who's just fine.	_____	_____
9. Something you wouldn't want to climb over.	_____	_____
10. An improved piece of outerwear.	_____	_____
11. When you say something very sad.	_____	_____
12. An aggressive adolescent.	_____	_____
13. A charming wind instrument.	_____	_____
14. A drawn-out musical number.	_____	_____
15. An ineffective place to hide from your enemy.	_____	_____
16. A tiny round plaything.	_____	_____
17. A silent uprising.	_____	_____
18. A funny urban locale.	_____	_____

Partial Word Bank

Emu, squirt, riot, flute, city, gazelle, wall, sweater, song, fort, small, spot, slum, remark, teen

The Lame Game #3

What's a fun activity you might not want to do? A "Lame Game." Answer each of the following clues below using two rhyming words. Some hints are provided, along with a partial word bank that provides half of the answer to each question.

1. A dirt-colored funny man	Brown	Clown
2. A boring youth.	Mild	_____
3. A decoration that is ready to eat.	_____	Stripe
4. A treatment for a very large bone fracture.	_____	_____
5. A brain for those who think nice thoughts.	_____	_____
6. Sweets you dropped at the beach.	_____	_____
7. What lets you into the ice rink.	_____	_____
8. A doily that looks like a person.	_____	_____
9. A small, furry, acorn-collecting female.	_____	_____
10. A geyser in the Rockies.	_____	_____
11. Where court jesters get an education.	_____	_____
12. When you use a spoon on Alphabet soup.	_____	_____
13. Something to take you away from a wedding.	_____	_____
14. A pickup in the mud.	_____	_____
15. An area with a purpose.	_____	_____
16. A wildlife preserve's grand opening.	_____	_____
17. The answer to smog and excessive garbage.	_____	_____
18. A health club with a pool.	_____	_____

Partial Word Bank

Lace, mountain, gate, gym, zoo, stuck, cast, candy, marriage, stirred, girl, kind, planned, solution, fool

The Lame Game #4

What's a fun activity you might not want to do? A "Lame Game." Answer each of the following clues below using two rhyming words. Some hints are provided, along with a partial word bank that provides half of the answer to each question.

1. A chef's answer to questions about seasoning	Spice	Advice
2. An animated lunar object	_____	Moon
3. Getting a good deal	Nice	_____
4. A bug's old-fashioned transportation.	_____	_____
5. A graphic design on your shopping vehicle.	_____	_____
6. A spot on your timepiece.	_____	_____
7. Minimalist art with only one-dimensional shapes.	_____	_____
8. A steel piece of cookware.	_____	_____
9. A letter covered in pentagrams.	_____	_____
10. A monster movie.	_____	_____
11. A frightening red berry.	_____	_____
12. It grows if you leave your bike outside in the winter.	_____	_____
13. Saying the wrong thing at the wrong time.	_____	_____
14. A lightly-colored jib.	_____	_____
15. An unexpected death.	_____	_____
16. The greatest nap you've ever taken.	_____	_____
17. A place where you can easily book your next holiday.	_____	_____
18. A bad place to buy a sandwich.	_____	_____

Partial word bank

smelly, lip, bicycle, art, metal, coach, feature, sail, surprise, vacation, card, design, blotch, cherry, best

The Lame Game #5

What's a fun activity you might not want to do? A "Lame Game." Answer each of the following clues below using two rhyming words. Some hints are provided, along with a partial word bank that provides half of the answer to each question.

1. Hamburger meat.	Ground	Round
2. A wall-hanging about thrill rides.	_____	Poster
3. The person who puts saltines in their boxes.	Cracker	_____
4. A purse full of treats.	_____	_____
5. A telephone ring in autumn.	_____	_____
6. A path that could collapse any moment.	_____	_____
7. A wrench-toting animal.	_____	_____
8. An arbor you don't need to pay for.	_____	_____
9. A blue-green marine animal.	_____	_____
10. A purplish body of water near islands.	_____	_____
11. A good place to put your food.	_____	_____
12. A city full of sad people.	_____	_____
13. You'd make one before buying a big screen.	_____	_____
14. A small, fake horse.	_____	_____
15. A letter pattern you can trace with lead.	_____	_____
16. A garden tool that isn't what it appears to be.	_____	_____
17. When you try out a happy facial expression.	_____	_____
18. Dirt made out of aluminum.	_____	_____

Partial word bank:

foil, fake, trail, pack, call, town, tool, trial, seal, stencil, maroon, phony, television, tree, table

The Lame Game #6

What's a fun activity you might not want to do? A "Lame Game." Answer each of the following clues below using two rhyming words. Some hints are provided, along with a partial word bank that provides half of the answer to each question.

1. Many cans of broth.	Soup	Troop
2. Where the rodents live.	_____	House
3. A flying group of pebbles.	Rock	_____
4. A large branch.	_____	_____
5. Little children's companion.	_____	_____
6. A tremor from your gastro-intestinal system.	_____	_____
7. A mysterious woman.	_____	_____
8. A calculating and elusive man.	_____	_____
9. A large trial piece.	_____	_____
10. A place to store your rocks.	_____	_____
11. A caravan of wheat.	_____	_____
12. Where a rodent, but not a mouse, might live.	_____	_____
13. A dark bag.	_____	_____
14. Difficult situations to discuss with others.	_____	_____
15. What you have if you've received a bachelor's.	_____	_____
16. A serpent after its nap.	_____	_____
17. An Elk's rear end.	_____	_____
18. A summertime dirigible.	_____	_____

Partial word bank:

grain, sly, ample, quiver, snake, caboose, twig, folder, hole, friend, balloon, sack, college, stuff, shady

The Lame Game #7

What's a fun activity you might not want to do? A "Lame Game." Answer each of the following clues below using two rhyming words. Some hints are provided, along with a partial word bank that provides half of the answer to each question.

1. A hot tempest.	Warm	Storm
2. The abilities of a blossom	_____	Power
3. A stepped-on fedora.	Flat	_____
4. An Upscale Restaurant.	_____	_____
5. A vegan's dinner choice.	_____	_____
6. A collection of forgotten tasks.	_____	_____
7. A fast elevator.	_____	_____
8. Pork from a Caribbean island.	_____	_____
9. A place to sit in Paris.	_____	_____
10. A code from Cairo.	_____	_____
11. Fast-working glue makes this.	_____	_____
12. An angry supervisor.	_____	_____
13. ...And seven years ago.	_____	_____
14. What a soldier or general might want.	_____	_____
15. A book about garden statues.	_____	_____
16. Where everyone's paychecks are put on display.	_____	_____
17. When it's time to get yourself clean.	_____	_____
18. An elephant could be described this way.	_____	_____

Partial word bank:

stick, salary, Egyptian, gnome, war, diner, list, hour, boss, swift, steak, bacon, French, hose, four

The Lame Game #8

What's a fun activity you might not want to do? A "Lame Game." Answer each of the following clues below using two rhyming words. Some hints are provided, along with a partial word bank that provides half of the answer to each question.

1. A wet puppy.	Soggy	Doggy
2. A magical snowstorm	Wizard	_____
3. A safe place for blackbirds.	_____	Haven
4. A funny Feline.	_____	_____
5. Leaves from this plant make a popular hot drink.	_____	_____
6. Something a bunny does every day.	_____	_____
7. A biologist's longwinded speech on flora.	_____	_____
8. An overnight airplane ride.	_____	_____
9. A king's chair made of granite.	_____	_____
10. A lunch-time eating instrument.	_____	_____
11. Difficult situations caused by soap in the air.	_____	_____
12. An abrupt poetic line.	_____	_____
13. A butler who notices everything.	_____	_____
14. The power driving your chariot.	_____	_____
15. A quantity of wood.	_____	_____
16. The edge of the steel mill's property.	_____	_____
17. Extremely dehydrated clam soup.	_____	_____
18. A box of dishes.	_____	_____

Partial word bank:

habit, powder, verse, plate, number, foundry, spoon, bubble, servant, stone, night, rant, witty, tea, horse

Word Squares #1

Find words by moving from any one starting square to any adjoining square. In each puzzle, you'll be searching for words which are at least three letters long that fit the theme of each puzzle. You may move up and down, left or right, or on a diagonal. Do not use any letters twice in the same word.

L	L	I	T	B
C	O	A	E	O
S	G	R	G	X
P	U	R	L	E
A	N	I	E	R

There are six types of dogs here.

Ten poetry types can be found in this one

N	P	R	S	T	P
K	C	O	D	E	I
A	K	I	N	N	C
I	U	Q	N	F	O
N	H	Y	M	P	U
U	G	E	L	E	T

S	T	G	S	F	P
E	G	E	R	T	R
K	A	R	O	I	Y
M	C	D	T	E	S
S	A	C	A	P	H
R	O	L	M	R	G

There are thirteen food words in this puzzle.

Word Squares #2

Find words by moving from any one starting square to any adjoining square. In each puzzle, you'll be searching for words which are at least three letters long that fit the theme of each puzzle. You may move up and down, left or right, or on a diagonal. Do not use any letters twice in the same word.

S	K	N	S	U
T	K	U	H	M
N	B	E	R	A
A	L	O	E	H
R	P	O	M	D

There are eleven things you might find in the forest in this puzzle.

Find the nine things you might see at a car race in this puzzle.

C	A	E	N	I	C
S	R	S	N	G	A
H	W	E	T	S	R
P	E	G	M	U	N
A	S	E	A	F	R
M	V	N	L	C	T

F	R	U	T	S	A
A	E	I	L	H	P
R	M	S	R	O	W
G	A	N	A	C	H
P	I	B	E	N	E
H	T	I	F	L	D

There are sixteen farming words in this puzzle.

Word Squares #3

Find words by moving from any one starting square to any adjoining square. In each puzzle, you'll be searching for words which are at least three letters long that fit the theme of each puzzle. You may move up and down, left or right, or on a diagonal. Do not use any letters twice in the same word.

A	O	G	E	C
D	T	U	R	A
G	E	L	T	B
C	K	A	N	I
R	O	S	H	L

There are 11 types of pets in this puzzle.

There are fourteen boy's names in this puzzle.

T	H	P	M	E	S
L	E	L	I	A	V
A	H	A	J	K	E
W	L	R	O	H	T
I	L	A	R	N	S
T	I	M	V	Y	E

There are twelve girl's names to be found here.

P	M	R	O	V	I
A	Y	J	A	C	K
T	T	E	N	M	I
C	S	U	N	R	A
L	T	E	R	A	G
K	A	I	N	C	Y

Word Squares #4

Find words by moving from any one starting square to any adjoining square. In each puzzle, you'll be searching for words which are at least three letters long that fit the theme of each puzzle. You may move up and down, left or right, or on a diagonal. Do not use any letters twice in the same word.

M	T	F	P	S
Q	A	L	I	E
U	N	R	L	N
R	S	E	C	H
A	T	V	M	O

Eight words about outer space can be seen here.

There are nine types of birds in this puzzle

D	P	E	N	A	V
U	F	G	O	R	E
C	R	S	O	I	N
K	I	E	L	B	N
T	N	R	A	P	A
W	O	C	R	S	W

Find all ten flower names in this puzzle.

B	U	T	T	E	R
M	M	E	P	U	C
F	S	O	B	L	O
I	T	R	N	B	I
R	A	C	Y	L	P
D	I	H	L	I	A

Word Squares #5

Find words by moving from any one starting square to any adjoining square. In each puzzle, you'll be searching for words which are at least three letters long that fit the theme of each puzzle. You may move up and down, left or right, or on a diagonal. Do not use any letters twice in the same word.

W	A	S	W	I
V	T	O	E	M
E	R	C	L	M
S	A	N	R	I
P	B	D	G	N

Find 6 words relating to the beach in this puzzle.

There are eight recent presidents hidden in this word square.

C	L	I	F	R	E
E	N	O	B	A	G
K	T	N	M	A	N
Y	D	E	B	I	X
R	B	U	S	H	O
O	F	N	O	N	J

There are 11 words related to picnics here

D	N	L	A	N	R
W	B	A	S	K	E
I	P	F	R	E	T
C	H	S	T	U	R
N	I	N	A	I	K
M	C	L	E	D	S

Word Squares #6

Find words by moving from any one starting square to any adjoining square. In each puzzle, you'll be searching for words which are at least three letters long that fit the theme of each puzzle. You may move up and down, left or right, or on a diagonal. Do not use any letters twice in the same word.

G	O	S	H	O
L	A	C	C	M
L	B	T	E	R
D	E	H	N	U
F	I	O	O	P

There are 8 sports words here.

Find the 8 jobs hidden in this puzzle.

P	R	O	Y	A	M
O	U	C	C	H	E
L	N	T	A	N	R
I	F	E	I	W	T
C	O	R	O	L	A
E	U	N	S	E	S

F	R	I	R	Y	A
M	D	Y	E	H	D
W	S	A	P	O	I
E	T	R	M	L	Y
E	I	C	O	U	J
L	K	H	T	N	E

Eleven things you can find on a calendar can be found in this puzzle.

Word Squares #7

Find words by moving from any one starting square to any adjoining square. In each puzzle, you'll be searching for words which are at least three letters long that fit the theme of each puzzle. You may move up and down, left or right, or on a diagonal. Do not use any letters twice in the same word.

M	U	C	T	P
I	S	L	H	M
E	C	E	E	A
N	G	L	R	T
C	E	I	S	H

There are 6 school subjects here:

Find the 8 bodily organs in this puzzle:

Y	C	E	P	S	F
O	L	E	L	I	V
U	V	O	N	R	E
N	I	C	R	T	S
G	H	E	A	I	T
X	O	B	N	M	O

Find the eight mythical creatures hidden here:

T	O	M	D	W	I
A	N	L	F	A	Z
U	E	I	E	R	D
R	C	G	M	O	N
C	Y	N	O	C	U
L	O	P	S	I	N

Word Squares #8

Find words by moving from any one starting square to any adjoining square. In each puzzle, you'll be searching for words which are at least three letters long that fit the theme of each puzzle. You may move up and down, left or right, or on a diagonal. Do not use any letters twice in the same word.

F	O	Y	M	E
P	R	E	N	S
K	C	H	T	A
U	N	I	B	E
G	A	O	R	D

There are 5 types of rooms in this puzzle:

Six of Shakespeare's plays can be found in this one:

E	S	R	M	K	I
P	T	O	R	A	N
H	M	U	T	E	G
A	L	E	H	I	L
C	B	L	O	J	U
K	O	A	N	D	T

H	C	C	N	G	R
I	B	R	O	T	A
O	E	L	I	I	V
W	H	L	N	Z	C
T	S	S	O	S	C
I	E	U	M	T	A

Eight types of pasta can be found here.

Missing Letters #1

The same single letter is missing from each of the scrambled circles below. Find the letter that you can include in each, and unscramble each word.

The Missing Letter is

_____

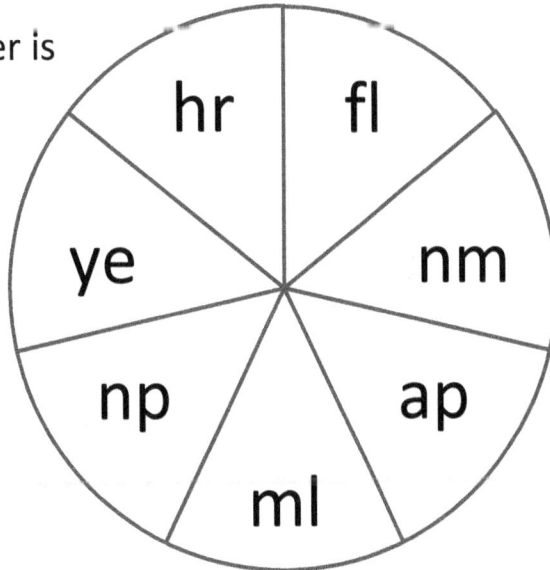

_____

_____

_____

_____

_____

_____

The Missing Letter is

_____

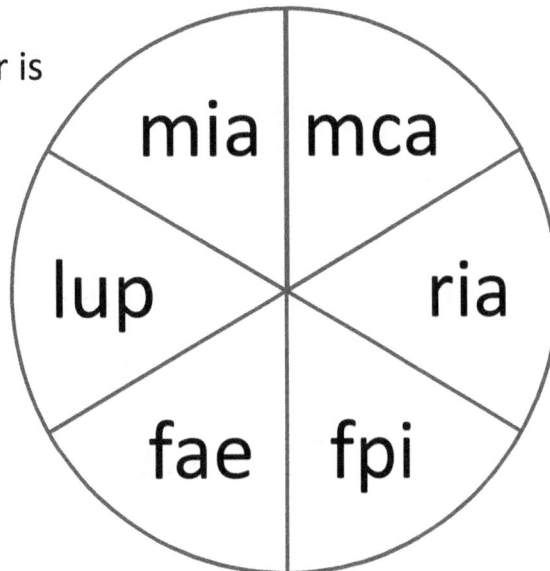

_____

_____

_____

_____

_____

_____

Missing Letters #2

The same single letter is missing from each of the scrambled circles below. Find the letter that you can include in each, and unscramble each word.

The Missing Letter is

_____

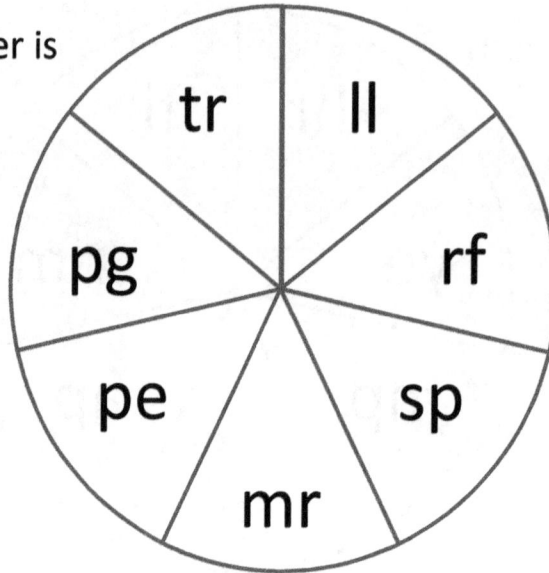

_____

_____

_____

_____

_____

_____

The Missing Letter is

_____

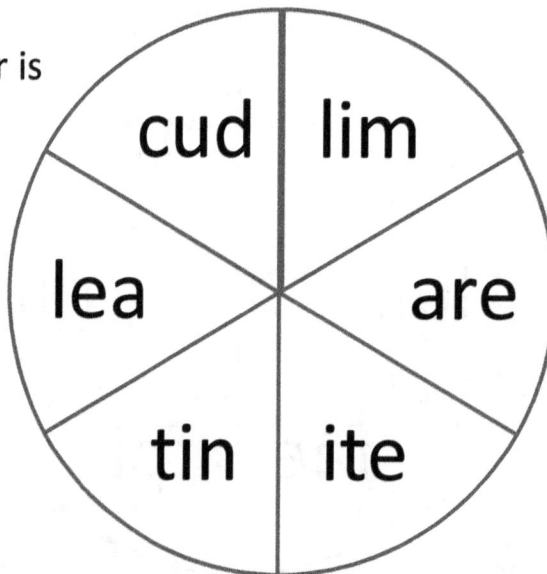

_____

_____

_____

_____

_____

Missing Letters #3

The same single letter is missing from each of the scrambled circles below. Find the letter that you can include in each, and unscramble each word.

The Missing Letter is

_____

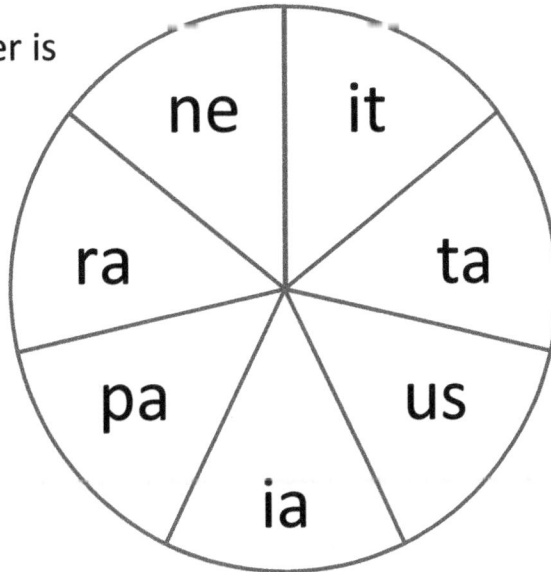

_____

_____

_____

_____

_____

_____

The Missing Letter is

_____

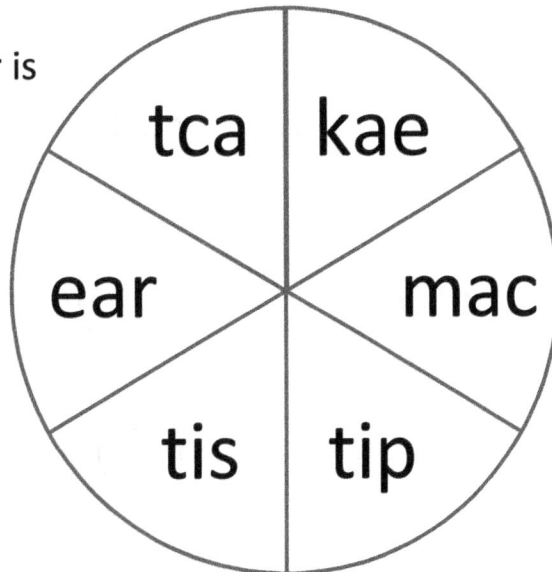

_____

_____

_____

_____

_____

Missing Letters #4

The same single letter is missing from each of the scrambled circles below. Find the letter that you can include in each, and unscramble each word.

The Missing Letter is

_____

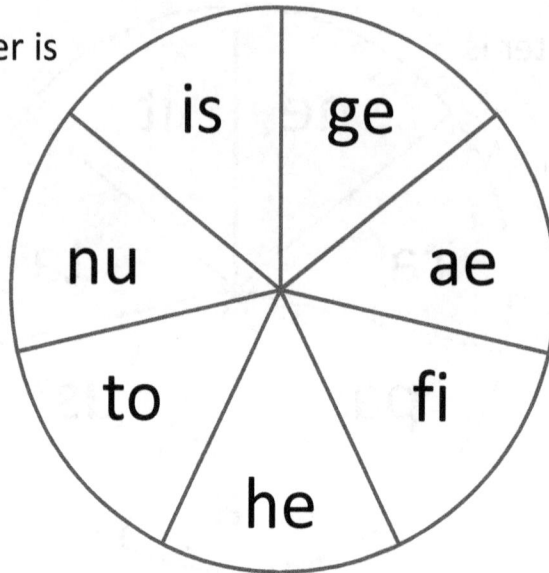

_____

_____

_____

_____

_____

_____

The Missing Letter is

_____

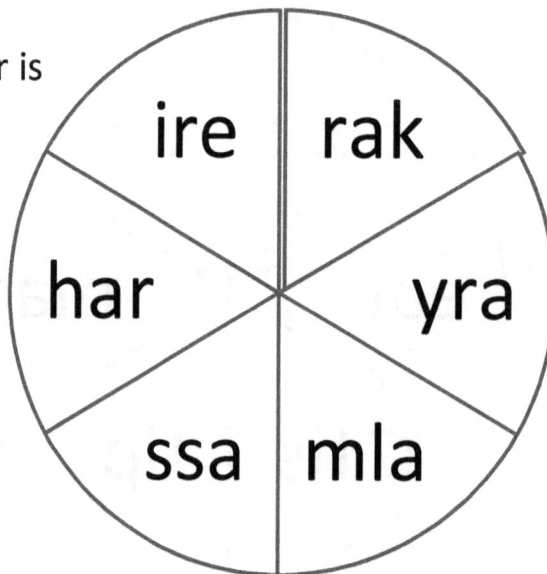

_____

_____

_____

_____

_____

Missing Letters #5

The same single letter is missing from each of the scrambled circles below. Find the letter that you can include in each, and unscramble each word.

The Missing Letter is

_____

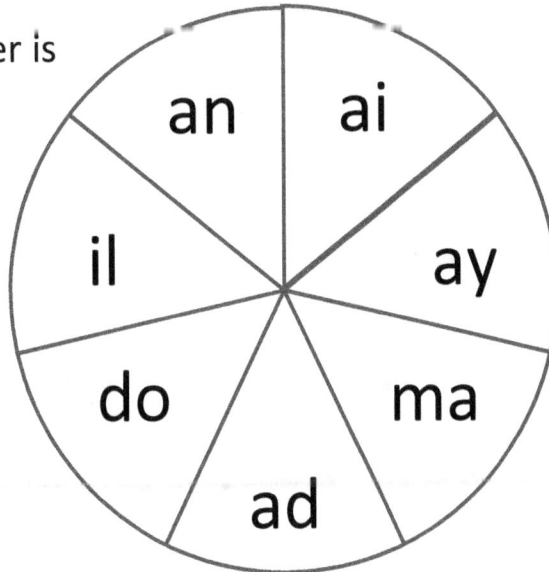

_____

_____

_____

_____

_____

_____

The Missing Letter is

_____

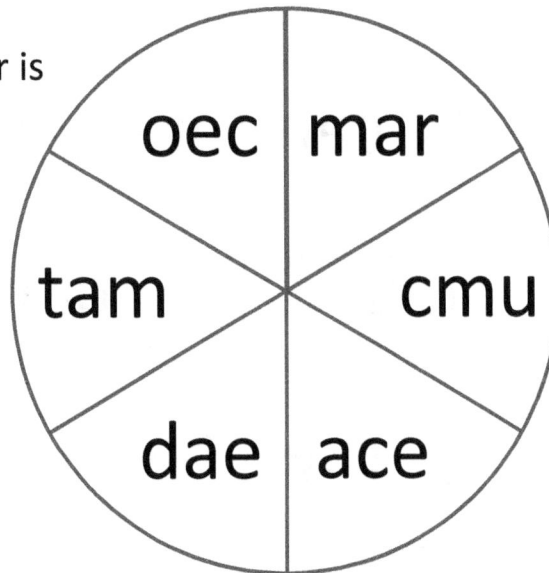

_____

_____

_____

_____

_____

Missing Letters #6

The same single letter is missing from each of the scrambled circles below. Find the letter that you can include in each, and unscramble each word.

The Missing Letter is

_____

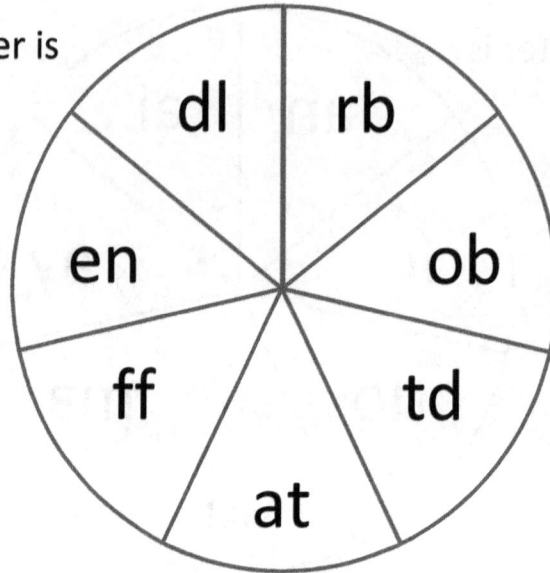

_____

_____

_____

_____

_____

_____

The Missing Letter is

_____

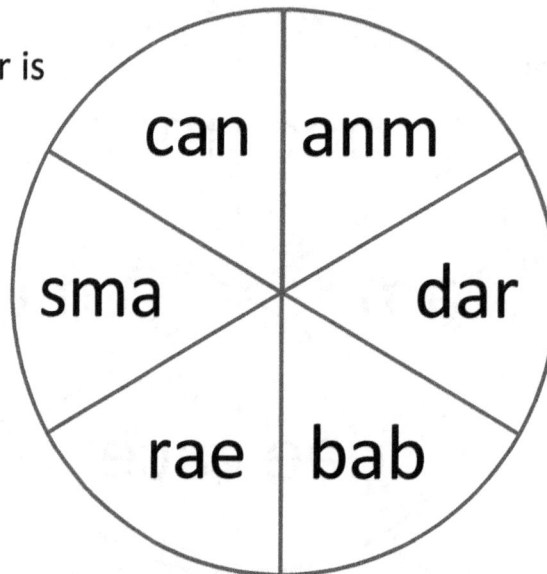

_____

_____

_____

_____

_____

Missing Letters #7

The same single letter is missing from each of the scrambled circles below. Find the letter that you can include in each, and unscramble each word.

The Missing Letter is

_____

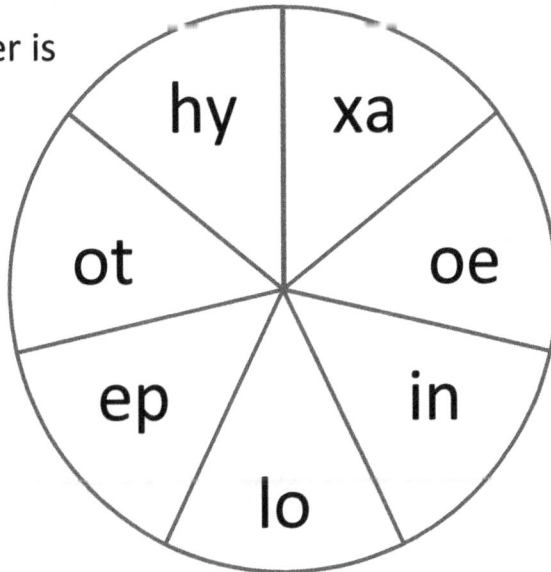

_____

_____

_____

_____

_____

_____

The Missing Letter is

_____

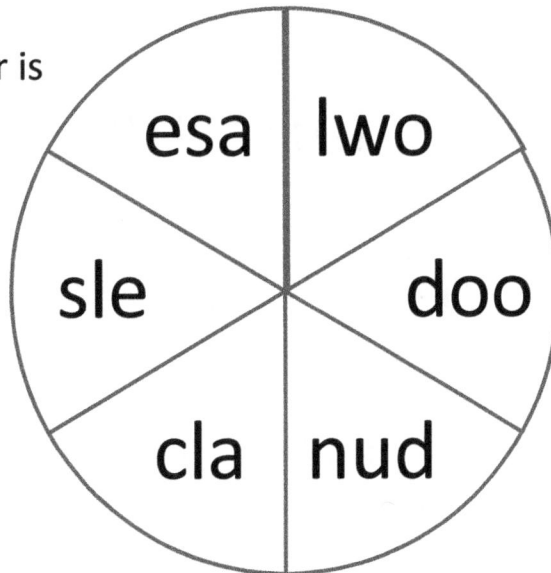

_____

_____

_____

_____

_____

Missing Letters #8

The same single letter is missing from each of the scrambled circles below. Find the letter that you can include in each, and unscramble each word.

The Missing Letter is

_____

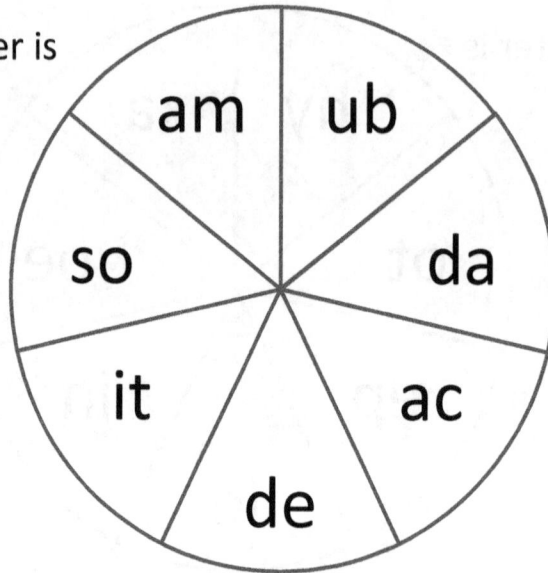

_____

_____

_____

_____

_____

_____

The Missing Letter is

_____

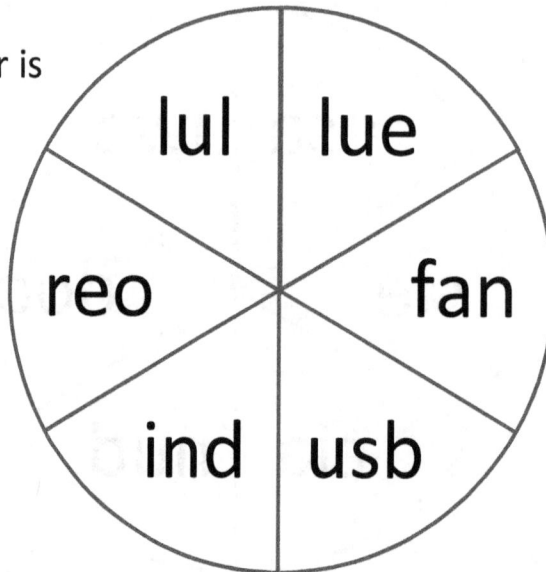

_____

_____

_____

_____

_____

Answer Keys

Word Ladder #1 – toad, road, read, rear, fear, feat, flat, flag, flan, flat, flap, slap, slam, slim, skim, skis, skit, spit, spin

Word Ladder #2 – loan, load, lord, lard, card, cord, cold, fold, ford, fore, yore, York, fork, cork, corn, morn, more, core

Word Ladder #3 – feel, feet, felt, melt, meld, mold, told, cold, cole, cola, hola, hold, held, head, lead, leak, beak, bean

Word Ladder #4 – clot, slot, slop, slap, clap, clad, glad, goad, goat, moat, molt, mold, mole, hole, hope, cope, cape, caps

Word Ladder #5 – book, boot, bolt, belt, welt, well, sell, seal, teal, team, tram, gram, gray, tray, trap, trip, grip, grim

Word Ladder #6 – rock, sock, sack, rack, race, lace, lame, lime, limp, wimp, wisp, wasp, wash, sash, sass, pass, past, mast

Word Ladder #7 – lets, jets, juts, buts, bunt, bent, tent, tend, mend, mens, mess, mass, pass, past, last, lust, just

Word Ladder #8 – salt, sale, same, name, Nome, none, cone, cane, cant, pant, part, port, fort, fork, folk, Polk, pole, role

Double Word Ladder #1 – hard, hold, helm, kelp, keys, rays, rain, hail, fall, male, mild, silk, mink, many, lane, hare, hone

Double Word Ladder #2 – fork, foam, road, glad, glue, flub, blue, true, tour, town, cows, cats, mits, milk, sulk, silo, halo

Double Word Ladder #3 – star, seat, silt, milk, mint, dent, left, soft, sold, colt, fold, mild, mall, hill, halt, melt, meal, fear

Double Word Ladder #4 – hope, cops, pups, pull, dell, felt, foot, foul, maul, maps, hops, home, hare, make, muse, moss, mist, kiss

Double Word Ladder #5 – coat, cold, card, mark, muck, dunk, sink, sits, oats, oops, rope, roil, sail, paul, aunt, suns, mums

Double Word Ladder #6 – mite, mane, cans, camp, lump, loop, boom, beam, best, rust, mutt, mart, jars, jets, beth, bash, bald, bird

Double Word Ladder #7 – flood, aloof, alone, stone, stung, young, youth, month, minty, pints, parts, pouts, pluto, plate, skate, spade, spuds, souls

Double Word Ladder #8 – style, still, stiff, cliff, climb, crime, gripe, grace, track, thick, thank, clank, blink, sling, slime, blame, beams, jeans

Lame Game #1 – 1. Cook book, 2. Fruit boot, 3. Hairy fairy, 4. Better letter, 5. Stale tale, 6. Frog bog, 7. Smart heart, 8. Phone loan, 9. Meeker speaker, 10. Met debt, 11. Red lead, 12. Mellow fellow, 13. Legal eagle, 14. Tile style, 15. Smelling dwelling, 16. Moo crew, 17. Great debate, 18. Flipper slipper

Lame Game #2 – 1. Merry berry, 2. Sock lock, 3. Glad dad, 4. Emu stew, 5. Hot spot, 6. Shirt squirt, 7. Slum drum, 8. Swell gazelle, 9. Tall wall, 10. Better sweater, 11. Dark remark, 12. Mean teen, 13. Cute flute, 14. Long song, 15. Short fort, 16. Small ball, 17. Quiet riot, 18. Witty city

Lame Game #3 – 1. Brown clown, 2. Mild child, 3. Ripe stripe, 4. Vast cast, 5. Kind mind, 6. Sandy candy, 7. Skate gate, 8. Lace face, 9. Squirrel girl, 10. Mountain fountain, 11. Fool school, 12. Stirred word, 13. Marriage Carriage, 14. Stuck truck, 15. Planned land, 16. New zoo, 17. Pollution solution, 18. Swim gym

Lame Game #4 – 1. Spice advice, 2. Cartoon moon, 3. Nice price, 4. Roach coach, 5. Cart art, 6. Watch blotch, 7. Line design, 8. Metal kettle, 9. Starred card, 10. Creature feature, 11. Scary cherry, 12. Bicycle icicle, 13. Lip slip, 14. Pale sail, 15. Surprise demise, 16. Best rest, 17. Vacation station, 18. Smelly deli

Lame Game #5 – 1. Ground round, 2. Coaster poster, 3. Cracker packer, 4. Snack pack, 5. Fall call, 6. Frail trail, 7. Tool mule, 8. Free tree, 9. Teal seal, 10. Maroon lagoon, 11. Stable table, 12. Frown town (or Down town), 13. Television decision, 14. Phony pony, 15. Pencil stencil, 16. Fake rake, 17. Trial smile, 18. Foil soil

Lame Game #6 – 1. Soup troop, 2. Mouse house, 3. Rock flock, 4. Big twig, 5. Pretend friend, 6. Liver quiver, 7. Shady lady, 8. Sly guy, 9. Ample sample, 10. Boulder folder, 11. Grain train, 12. Mole hole, 13. Black sack, 14. Tough stuff, 15. College knowledge, 16. Awake snake, 17. Moose caboose, 18. June balloon

Lame Game #7 – 1. Warm storm, 2. Flower power, 3. Flat hat, 4. Finer diner, 5. Fake steak, 6. Missed list, 7. Swift lift, 8. Jamaican bacon, 9. French bench, 10. Egyptian encryption, 11. Quick stick, 12. Cross boss, 13. Four score, 14. More war, 15. Gnome tome, 16. Salary gallery, 17. Shower hour, 18. Hose nose

Lame Game #8 – 1. Soggy Doggy, 2. Wizard Blizzard, 3. Raven Haven, 4. Witty Kitty, 5. Tea Tree, 6. Rabbit Habit, 7. Plant Rant, 8. Night Flight, 9. Stone Throne, 10. Noon Spoon, 11. Bubble Trouble, 12. Terse Verse, 13. Observant Servant, 14. Horse Force, 15. Lumber Number, 16. Foundry Boundary, 17. Powder Chowder, 18. Plate Crate

Word Squares #1
Dogs: beagle, terrier, boxer, pug, spaniel, collie
Poems: acrostic, cinquain, haiku, elegy, epic, hymn, ode, prose, sonnet,couplet
Foods: steak, fries, eggs, cream, stirfry, carrot, cake, cola, tea, dates, grapes, tacos

Word Squares #2
Forest: shrub, hare, bush, plant, deer, skunk, mushroom, bee, ants, bloom, sun
Racetrack: cars, flags, pavement, turns, fans, crash, wheel, engines, racing
Farm: farmer, fence, cow, pasture, horse, field, grain, ranch, corn, silo, beans, barn, rain, pig, fruit, crow

Word Squares #3
Pets: snake, dog, cat, gecko, turtle, crab, gerbil, rat, rock, bat
Boys: Mike, Steve, Ralph, John, Elijah, Tim, William, Jim, Harry, Walt, Larry, Marv, Ron
Girls: Sue, Mary, Jane, Anne, Claire, Kate, Vicki, Patty, Margaret, Joan, Pam, Nancy

Word Squares #4
Space: Mars, sun, Venus, star, eclipse, alien, flare, comet
Birds: crow, duck, swan, robin, penguin, sparrow, oriole, goose
Flowers: iris, buttercup, mums, tulip, bulb, orchid, dahlia, peony, lily

Word Squares #5
Beach: sand, waves, water, crabs, towel, swimming
Presidents: Reagan, Clinton, Ford, Johnson, Obama, Nixon, Bush, Kennedy
Picnic: picnic, basket, blanket, sandwich, chips, kids, park, tree, fruit, nature, ants

Word Squares #6
Sports: goal, field, soccer, homerun, bat, ball, net, hoop
Jobs: police, accountant, mayor, counselor, sales, waiter, teacher, nurse
Calendar: dates, March, April, June, July, days, Friday, year, month, week, holiday

Word Squares #7
Classes: math, music, science, English, theatre, art
Organs: stomach, spleen, liver, intestine, heart, lung, voicebox, colon
Mythological creatures: minotaur, centaur, gnome, elf, dwarf, wizard, unicorn, cyclops

Word Squares #8
Rooms: Foyer, kitchen, porch, bedroom, basement
Shakespeare: King Lear, Macbeth, Othello, Hamlet, Romeo and Juliet, Tempest
Pasta: Elbows, shells, ravioli, rotini, ziti, bowties, mostaccioli, gnocchi

Missing Letters #1
Puzzle 1: The missing letter is 'e'. The words are men, elf, ape, pen, her, eye, her and elm.
Puzzle 2: The missing letter is 'l'. The words are calm (or clam), flip, leaf, mail, pull and rail (or lair or liar).

Missing Letters #2
Puzzle 1: The missing letter is 'a'. The words are ape (or pea), all, spa, arm (or ram), tar (or rat) and gap.
Puzzle 2: The missing letter is 'k'. The words are milk, rake, kite, leak (or kale), knit, and duck.

Missing Letters #3
Puzzle 1: The missing letter is 'm'. The words are mit, mat, sum, aim, map (or amp), and ram (or arm).
Puzzle 2: The missing letter is 'r'. The words are rake, cram, trip, stir, rare (or rear), and cart.

Missing Letters #4

Puzzle 1: The missing letter is 't'. The words are get, fit, ate (or tea), tar (or rat), the, lot, nut and sit.

Puzzle 2: The missing letter is 'p'. The words are park, lamp (or palm), saps (or pass), pray, harp, and ripe.

Missing Letters #5

Puzzle 1: The missing letter is 'd'. The words are and, aid, day, add (or dad), odd, lid, and dam.

Puzzle 2: The missing letter is 'h'. The words are echo, harm, much, ache, head, and math.

Missing Letters #6

Puzzle 1: The missing letter is 'o'. The words are old, orb, boo, dot, oat, off, and one

Puzzle 2: The missing letter is 'y'. The words are many, yard, baby, year, cyan and yams.

Missing Letters #7

Puzzle 1: The missing letter is 'w'. The words are wax, two (or tow), owe, pew, owl, win and why.

Puzzle 2: The missing letter is 'f'. The words are fowl, safe, food, calf, fund and self.

Missing Letters #8

Puzzle 1: The missing letter is 'n'. The words are bun (or nub), man, and, can, den (or end), tin and son.

Puzzle 2: The missing letter is 'g'. The words are gull, glue, fang, bugs, ding, and gore.

Templates

Word Ladders

Word ladder puzzles were invented by Lewis Carroll, the author of Alice in Wonderland, among other books. These kinds of puzzles are designed to test your vocabulary and reasoning skills. In each puzzle, you must change just one letter from the line above to create a new word that fits the clue. The first one is started for you.

＿ ＿ ＿ ＿	
＿ ＿ ＿ ＿	
＿ ＿ ＿ ＿	
＿ ＿ ＿ ＿	
＿ ＿ ＿ ＿	
＿ ＿ ＿ ＿	
＿ ＿ ＿ ＿	
＿ ＿ ＿ ＿	
＿ ＿ ＿ ＿	
＿ ＿ ＿ ＿	
＿ ＿ ＿ ＿	
＿ ＿ ＿ ＿	
＿ ＿ ＿ ＿	
＿ ＿ ＿ ＿	
＿ ＿ ＿ ＿	
＿ ＿ ＿ ＿	

The Lame Game

What's a fun activity you might not want to do? A "Lame Game." Answer each of the following clues below using two rhyming words. Some hints are provided.

1.	
2.	
3.	
4.	
5.	
6.	
7.	
8.	
9.	
10.	
11.	
12.	
13.	
14.	
15.	
16.	
17.	
18.	

Word Squares

Find words by moving from any one starting square to any adjoining square. In each puzzle, you'll be searching for words which are at least three letters long that fit the theme of each puzzle. You may move up and down, left or right, or on a diagonal. Do not use any letters twice in the same word.

Describe the topic here.

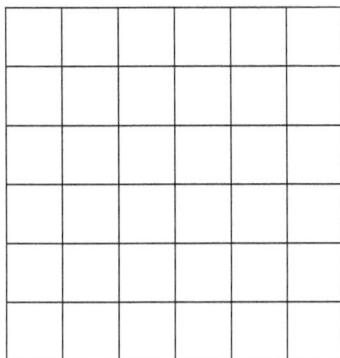

Describe the topic here.

Describe the topic here.

Missing Letters

The same single letter is missing from each of the scrambled circles below. Find the letter that you can include in each, and unscramble each word.

The Missing Letter is

_____

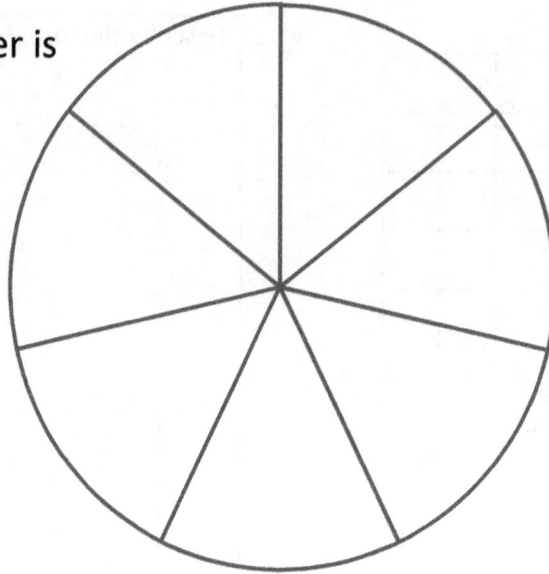

_____

_____

_____

_____

_____

_____

_____

The Missing Letter is

_____

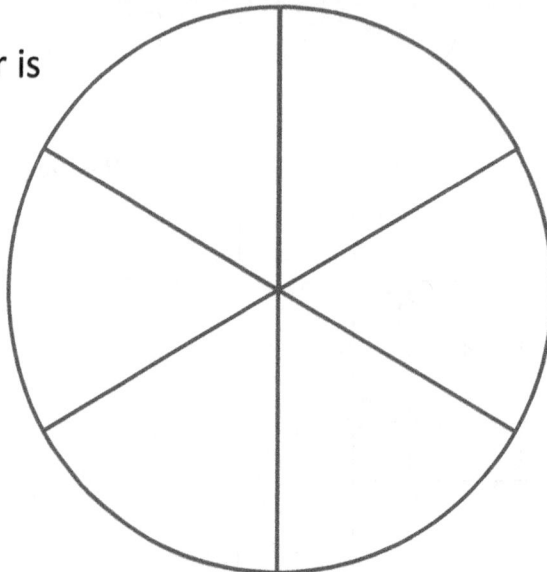

_____

_____

_____

_____

_____

_____

www.ingramcontent.com/pod-product-compliance
Lightning Source LLC
LaVergne TN
LVHW061249060426
835508LV00018B/1557